GULLIVER

1022

Terence Blacker, geboren 1948 in Suffolk, versuchte sich nach dem Studium als Jockey und Buchhändler und war danach im Verlagswesen tätig. Seit 1983 widmet er sich als Autor, Journalist und Kolumnist ganz dem Schreiben. Er lebt mit seiner Familie in London. Bei Beltz & Gelberg erschienen 15 Bände der erfolgreichen Miss-Wiss-Serie sowie der Roman *Boy2Girl*.

Tony Ross, geboren 1938 in London, gehört zu den international bekanntesten Kinder- und Jugendbuchillustratoren und wurde mit zahlreichen Preisen ausgezeichnet. Bei Beltz & Gelberg illustrierte er u.a. Eoin Colfers Kinderromane *Tim und das Geheimnis von Knolle Murphy* und *Tim und das Geheimnis von Captain Crow*.

Terence Blacker

Charming Miss Wiss

Illustrated by
Tony Ross

Glossary included

GULLIVER
von BELTZ & Gelberg

www.gulliver-welten.de
Gulliver 1022
Originalausgabe

Die englische Originalausgabe erschien 1996 u.d.T.
Ms Wiz spells Trouble bei Macmillan Children's Books, London
Textbearbeitung und Glossar: Jane Rösel
Layout: Julia Rissler
Einbandgestaltung: Max Bartholl
Einbandbild: Tony Ross
Gesamtherstellung: Beltz Druckpartner GmbH & Co. KG,
Hemsbach
Printed in Germany
ISBN 978-3-407-74022-9
3 4 5 15 14 13

CHAPTER ONE
The New Teacher

Most teachers are strange. The teachers at St Barnabas School were strange too. Mr Gilbert, the head teacher, liked to pick his nose during **Assembly**. Mrs Hicks talked to her teddies in class. Miss Gomaz smoked cigarettes in the toilet. But Class Three's new teacher was the strangest.
Some of the children in Class Three thought she was a **witch**. Others said she was a hippy. A few of them thought she was just a bit crazy.

assembly: Schulversammlung (morgens) –
witch: Hexe

St Barnabas had never had a teacher like her before.

This is her story. What do *you* think she was?

The new teacher walked into the classroom on the first day of school. The children of Class Three knew there was something different about her. She was tall, with long black hair and bright green eyes. She wore tight jeans and a purple blouse. She wore lots of large rings and black **nail varnish**. She looked like a disco dancer, not like a school teacher.
The biggest surprise of all was that she wasn't nervous. Class Three was called

nail varnish: Nagellack

the "problem class". Some teachers said children were difficult and noisy. Miss Jones, their last teacher, had left the school crying.

"My name is Miss Wisdom," she said quietly. "So what do you say to me every morning when I walk in?"

"Good morning, Miss Wisdom," said Class Three bored.

"Wrong," said the teacher with a flash of her green eyes, "You say *Good morning, charming Miss Wiss!* And I will say, *Good morning, wonderful Class Three.*"

Jack, who was one of Class Three's louder boys, **giggled** at the back of the class.

to giggle: kichern

"Yo," he said in a silly American accent. "No problem!"

"And why charming?" asked a large boy sitting in the front row. It was Podge, who was the **greediest** boy in the class.

"Charming?" said Miss Wiss with a mysterious smile. "Just you wait and see."

Miss Wiss had put a big leather bag beside her desk. She put her hand inside and pulled out a **china** cat.

"That," she said, putting the cat on her desk, "is my friend Hecate the Cat. She's watching you all the time. She sees everything and hears everything. She's my **spy**."

greedy: gierig – **china:** Porzellan – **spy:** Spion

Miss Wiss turned to the blackboard.
"**Weird**," **muttered** Jack.
A **strange**, **hissing** sound came from the china cat. Its eyes lit up like **torches**.
"Hecate sees you even when my back is turned," said Miss Wiss, looking at the class. "Will the person who said *weird* please **spell** it?"
Everyone stared at Jack. His face went red.
"I. T.," he **stammered**.
No one laughed.
"Er, W… I…"
"Wrong," said Miss Wiss. "W.E.I.R.D.
If you don't know how to spell a word,

weird: merkwürdig – **to mutter:** murmeln – **strange:** seltsam – **torch:** Taschenlampe, Fackel – **to spell:** buchstabieren – **to stammer:** stottern – **to hiss:** fauchen, zischen – **to pat**: tätscheln

Jack, don't use it." She **patted** the china cat.
"Good girl, Hecate," she said.
"How did she know my name?" whispered Jack.
The new teacher smiled. "Children, remember one thing. Miss Wiss knows everything."
"Now," she said. "Pay attention, please.

Talking of spelling, I'm going to give you a first lesson in **casting spells**. That's magic."

"Oh great," said Katrina **grumpily**. "Our teacher is a witch!"

Hecate the Cat hissed.

"No, Katrina, not a witch," said Miss Wiss. "We don't call them witches these days. It gives people the wrong idea. We call them ***Paranormal Operatives***. Now what shall be our first spell?"

Podge put up his hand.

"Could we turn our **crayons** into lollipops, please Miss Wiss?" he asked.

"No," said Miss Wiss. "Spells are not **for personal greed**."

to cast a spell: jemanden/etwas verzaubern – **grumpily:** mürrisch – **Paranormal Operatives:** Fachfrau für Übersinnliches – **crayon:** Buntstift – **for personal greed:** aus persönlicher Gier

"How about turning Class Two into frogs?" asked Katrina.

"Nor are they **for revenge**. There will be no **unpleasant** spells around here while I'm your teacher," said Miss Wiss before she added: "Only if we absolutely must, of course."

She looked out of the window. In the playground Mr Brown, the school **caretaker**, was **sweeping up** leaves.

"Please draw a picture of the playground," said Miss Wiss. "Without any leaves. The best picture will create the spell."

Almost for the first time ever, Class Three worked without saying a word.

for revenge: aus Rache – **unpleasant:** unangenehm – **caretaker:** Hausmeister – **to sweep up:** zusammen-kehren

Katrina didn't **complain** that someone had taken her pencil. Caroline concentrated on her work. Podge forgot to look in his jeans pocket for a

to complain: sich beschweren – **pellet:** Kugel

sweet. Jack did not shoot any paper **pellets** across the room.
At the end of the lesson, Miss Wiss looked at the drawings.
"Well, they're all quite good," she said after a while. "But I think I like Caroline's the best."

She took Caroline's drawing and **taped** it to the window with sticky tape.
"Please close your eyes while I cast the spell," she said.
There was a strange **humming noise** as Class Three sat, eyes closed, in silence.
"Open," said Miss Wiss, after a few seconds. "Look at Caroline's work."
The children looked at Caroline's drawing. It was **steaming** a little bit. In one corner there was a **pile** of leaves.
"Hey – look at the playground!" shouted Katrina.
Everyone looked out of the window and they were amazed. There were no more

to tape: kleben – **humming noise:** leises Summen – **to steam:** dampfen – **pile:** Haufen – **wheelbarrow:** Schubkarren – **to scratch:** kratzen

leaves on the ground – they had disappeared. Mr Brown stood by his **wheelbarrow**, **scratching** his head.
"Weird," said Jack. "Very weird indeed."

CHAPTER TWO
"Miss Wiss is Magic"

"Yes, she is a bit strange," said the head teacher, Mr Gilbert, as he was drinking a cup of tea one morning with Miss Gomaz and Mrs Hicks in the Teachers' Room.

"Those jeans," said Miss Gomaz with her nose in the air. "And the *black* nail-varnish. Here … At St Barnabas …"

"But she has Class Three under control," said Mr Gilbert. "She has been here a whole week and not one child has been sent to my office. Not one window has been broken."

Mrs Hicks **stirred** her tea with a sour look on her face. "It won't last," she said. "That class is too much to handle.

And there are some very strange noises coming from that classroom."
"Keep an eye on the situation please, Mr Gilbert," said Miss Gomaz.
"Yes," he said, "I will." Mr Gilbert sighed. He was tired.

to stir: rühren

The fact is that all of Class Three, including the difficult children, were having a wonderful time. Every lesson with Miss Wiss was different.

"Now, Class Three," she would say, "I'm going to teach you something a bit unusual. But remember – what happens in this classroom is our **secret**. The magic only works if nobody but us knows about it."

Class Three **agreed**.

So no one – not even parents or other children at the school – had any idea of the strange things that happened to Class Three.

They never heard how Caroline's picture of the playground helped Mr Brown do a morning's work.

secret: Geheimnis – **to agree:** zustimmen – **by itself:** von selbst – **vacuum cleaner:** Staubsauger

They never heard how Jack's desk moved to the front of the class all **by itself** when Hecate saw him talking at the back of the room.
They never heard how Katrina flew around the class three times on a **vacuum cleaner** after she had complained that Miss Wiss couldn't be

a real witch – sorry, Paranormal Operative – because she didn't ride a **broomstick**.

They never heard about the nature lesson when the class met Herbert,

a pet rat that Miss Wiss kept up her **sleeve**.
But they did hear about the day when Podge became the hero of the class. Nobody could keep *that* a secret.

Once every year, Class Three played a football match against a team from a nearby school, called Brackenhurst. It was a very important game and everyone from St Barnabas came to the playground to watch. Last year, Class Three had lost 10-0.
"That was because Miss Jones chose all the losers," explained Jack.
"Because she was a loser herself," said Caroline.

broomstick: Besen, Besenstiel – **sleeve:** Ärmel

The rest of the class agreed.
"*I'll* be manager," shouted Jack loudly.
Miss Wiss held up her hands like a wizard doing a magic trick.
"*I'll* be manager," she said.
"But you don't know anything about football," said Jack.
"Miss Wiss knows everything," said Caroline.
"**Creep!**" said Katrina.
Hecate the Cat hissed.
"All right, Hecate," said Katrina. "I'm sorry."
"My team," said Miss Wiss, "is Jack, Simon, Katrina, Alex and . . ."
She looked around the classroom and saw Podge's arm waving wildly.

creep: Mistkerl

"*No,* Miss Wiss," some of the class shouted together. "Not Podge! He's useless!"
". . . and Podge!"
The rest of the class **groaned**.
"We're going to lose again!" said Jack.

The St Barnabas team did not play well that afternoon. Maybe Jack would be right. Maybe they would lose again. Brackenhurst **scored** two times in the first three minutes. Podge was a disaster. He fell over his own feet when the ball came near him.
Mrs Hicks and Miss Gomaz smiled when they saw this. They did not like Miss Wiss. "Look at her, jumping up

to groan: stöhnen – **to score** (a goal): ein Tor schießen and down like that. She looks **silly** in front of the children. She is like a child herself."

"It's **embarrassing**," agreed Miss Gomaz.

"Do something," said Caroline who was standing next to Miss Wiss.

"And what should I do, Caroline?" asked Miss Wiss. Her face was quite red.

"You know," whispered Caroline. "Something special."

"Oh, all right," sighed Miss Wiss. "I suppose a *little* magic wouldn't hurt."

At that moment, Podge crashed into one of the Brackenhurst's players and knocked him over. Mr Gilbert was **referee**. He blew hard on his **whistle** for

silly: blöd – **embarrassing:** peinlich – **referee:** Schiedsrichter – **whistle:** Trillerpfeife

a free kick – but no sound came out. The only sound was a soft humming noise near Miss Wiss.

"That's better," said Caroline.

Brackenhurst's players waited for the whistle to blow. Podge started to run with the ball. He took two steps and kicked it wildly but it was nowhere near the Brackenhurst goal. Suddenly, the ball flew into the net. Podge scored a goal.

For a moment, everyone was shocked. Then Miss Wiss started to cheer.

“What a shot!” she shouted. “Nice one, Podge!”

“What behaviour!” muttered Mrs Hicks.

From then on, the game changed completely. Podge played like a champion. Better than in his dreams! Soon even Jack was shouting, “Give it to Podge! Give the ball to Podge!” The Brackenhurst players screamed, “Stop the fat one!”

But nobody could stop Podge. It was like magic. He scored three goals. Class Three won 3-2.

After the game, the class stood around Miss Wiss, shouting, cheering and singing songs.
"So she has her class under control, does she?" said Mrs Hicks. "They may win matches but Class Three have no discipline with the new teacher."
Miss Gomaz ran to Mr Gilbert.
"Look at that, head teacher," she said and pointed to Class Three. They were singing "Miss Wiss is magic!" But Mr Gilbert wasn't listening. He was still looking at his new whistle. "Why doesn't it work?" he **wondered**.

to wonder: sich fragen

CHAPTER THREE
An Extremely Mathematical **Owl**

"This is all very difficult," said Mr Gilbert, puffing nervously on his pipe. He was sitting in his office with Miss Wiss. "Very tricky. You see, Miss Wisdom – er, Miss Wiss – some people have complained."

"Oh my goodness," said Miss Wiss. "What is the matter?"

Mr Gilbert played around with his pipe. Why *was* he feeling so nervous? Of course, women always made him nervous – especially his wife, Mrs Gilbert. He sat up in his **armchair** and tried again.

owl: Eule – **armchair:** Sessel

"Firstly, some people don't like the way you look," he said, looking at Miss Wiss. She was wearing black **lipstick** today.
"Is there something wrong with the way I look?" asked Miss Wiss. She was confused.
"No, no," said Mr Gilbert, tapping his pipe on an **ashtray**, "I like . . . I mean, I don't . . . personally . . . Then," he quickly changed the subject. "What you teach . . . Your history lessons, for example."
"But Class Three loves history," said Miss Wiss. "We're doing the French Revolution at the moment."
"So I have heard," said Mr Gilbert. "The class was walking around the

lipstick: Lippenstift – **ashtray:** Aschenbecher

playground yesterday shouting, *Off with their heads!* Jack had a potato on a sharp stick."

Miss Wiss laughed. "They're very enthusiastic," she said.

"Perhaps you could look at some other part of history – *nice* history," said the head teacher. "1066, the Armada, King Alfred and the cakes."

"Oh no," said Miss Wiss. "We already have our next project."

"What is it?" asked Mr Gilbert worried.

"The Great Fire of London," said Miss Wiss.

The head teacher looked nervous again. Mrs Hicks and Miss Gomaz had been right. Miss Wiss was trouble.

"Perhaps," he said, "you could concentrate on some other subject for *now*."

"Of course," said Miss Wiss. "We'll do some maths for a while."
Mr Gilbert smiled for the first time that morning.
"Perfect," he said. Maths couldn't **cause trouble**. Could it? he wondered.

"Now, Class Three," said Miss Wiss that afternoon. "It is time for a test on your **nine times table** – multiplication and division."
There was a groan around the classroom. Nobody liked the nine times table.
"And to help me," said Miss Wiss, "I've brought my friend Archimedes."

to cause trouble: Ärger machen – **nine times table:** 9er-Reihe

Archimedes was a large white owl.
"Archie is what they call a *number-cruncher.* He loves his tables," she said, putting the owl on top of the blackboard.
"Cats, rats and now owls," muttered Katrina." Are we in a zoo?"
"Archie is a **barn owl**," said Miss Wiss, ignoring Katrina. "An extremely mathematical barn owl. Put the **waste-paper basket** beneath him please, Caroline."
"Why, Miss Wiss?" asked Caroline.
"Wait and see," said Miss Wiss.
Caroline put the waste-paper basket beneath Archie. The owl looked around the classroom, blinking wisely.

barn owl: Schleiereule – **waste-paper basket:** Papierkorb

"Now Podge," said Miss Wiss. "Tell Archie what five nines are."
"Forty-five," said Podge.
"Toowoo," said Archie.
"That means correct," said Miss Wiss. "Simon – nine nines."
"Eighty-one," said Simon.
"Toowoo."
"Now Jack," said Miss Wiss. "Let's try division. A boy has 108 **marbles**. He divides them among his nine friends. What does that make?"
"It makes him an idiot for giving away all his marbles," said Jack.
Archie looked confused.
"Try again, Jack," said Miss Wiss patiently.

marbles: Murmeln

"Err . . . eleven?"
Class Three looked at Archie. Without a sound, the owl lifted his tail and did something very **nasty** into the waste-paper basket beneath him.

"Uuuuuuuurrrggghhhh," said the children. "He's done a _____"

"The correct word is guano," said Miss Wiss. "Jack?"

"Ten?" said Jack.

Archie lifted his tail.

"Eight?"

Archie did it again.

"How does he do that?" asked Podge.

Miss Wiss **shrugged** her shoulders.

"He's well trained," she said.

"We need another basket," said Katrina. "Jack will never get it right."

nasty: scheußlich, grässlich

“He should,” said Miss Wiss. “Every time Archie has to do his . . . guano, it means you write fifty lines.”
Jack groaned. “Um. . .”

to shrug: Achsel zucken

Mrs Hicks and Miss Gomaz were listening outside the door. They had given their classes some reading work to do. They wanted to catch the new teacher doing something wrong.

"Listen to that terrible noise," said Miss Gomaz.

"Let's look through the window from the playground," said Mrs Hicks.
Moments later, the two teachers were watching as Jack tried hard to give Archie the correct answer.
"There's a bird on the blackboard," said Miss Gomaz.

"It's . . . it's going to the toilet," said Mrs Hicks, shocked. "In a bin!"
They pressed their noses to the window to see better.
Miss Wiss looked up and hummed softly.
"Miss Gomaz! Miss Gomaz!" said Mrs Hicks. "My nose! It's stuck to the glass!"
"Mine too!" cried Miss Gomaz, trying to pull back from the window-pane. "Ouch! That hurts!"
Just then the bell rang for afternoon break. Soon the children were standing around the two teachers, laughing at them.
"Don't just stand there, you horrible children," screamed Mrs Hicks. "Get help quickly!"
"No need," said Miss Wiss. She came to the children. She tapped the glass. Miss

Gomaz and Mrs Hicks fell to the ground. Free at last.
"Maybe it was the frost?" asked Miss Wiss, with a strange little smile.
"Frost?" said Miss Gomaz, rubbing her nose. "At this time of year? Don't talk rubbish! Rubbish!"
"It's only September," said Mrs Hicks.
"Yes," said Miss Wiss. "What funny weather we're having, don't you think?"

CHAPTER FOUR
Herbert Takes a Wrong Turning

Class Three wondered where Miss Wiss came from. In the art lesson that afternoon she gave them a **clue**.
She had asked the children to draw *The House of My Dreams.*
Jack drew a house that looked like Wembley Stadium. It had a **football pitch** in the living room and all the walls were like skateboard ramps.
Caroline drew the villa that she would have when she became a film star. It had a huge lawn and swimming pool. In every room there was a cocktail cabinet for drinks.

clue: Hinweis – **football pitch:** Fußballplatz

Podge drew Buckingham Palace made of chocolate and fudge.
Katrina drew a strange, dark **cottage** in a wood. Cats with shining eyes sat each side of the front door and bats flew in and out of its old **thatched roof**. She called it *Miss Wiss' Magic Cottage.*
When Katrina finished the picture, Miss Wiss laughed. "It's lovely," she said, "but not at all like where I really live."
"Where *do* you live?" asked Katrina. The class became quiet. No one had ever asked Miss Wiss about herself before.
"I live in a flat a long, long way away," said Miss Wiss. "None of you have ever been there, I'm sure. It's outside the town."

cottage: Häuschen, Hütte – **thatched roof:** Reetdach

"Can we come and visit you during the holidays?" asked Jack.
"During the holidays I'm doing other things," said Miss Wiss. "That's my job – to go wherever a little magic is needed."
"Does that mean you'll leave us soon?" said Katrina.
Miss Wiss smiled. "Katrina, I'll leave you when you no longer need me."
For a moment, there was silence in Class Three. Then Podge put up his hand.
"If you live so far away," he asked, "how do you get to school every day? Do you fly on your vacuum cleaner?"
"No," said Miss Wiss. "I come by bus."

Miss Wiss was more serious than usual that afternoon. She was thinking of the evening. It would be her first Parents'

Evening and she was nervous. Miss Wiss liked being with children. She liked being with teachers. But a whole evening with parents made her feel nervous.

"I must not do any magic tonight," she said to herself. "Adults aren't like children. Magic is a problem for them."

It was evening. The door opened.

"I'm Harris," said a large man in a suit. He was the first parent to arrive. He shook Miss Wiss by the hand. "Peter's dad. This is Mother." A nervous-looking woman stood a step behind him.

Peter? Who was Peter? Of course – that was Podge's real name.

"Pod – I mean Peter is doing well," she said, looking at her notes.

"We're not happy," said Mr Harris. "Isn't that right, Mother?"
"It is," said Mrs Harris. "We're not happy at all."
"The boy is strange," said Mr Harris. "Always got his head in a book. Or talking about school. Asking us questions about this and that when his mother and I are trying to watch **telly**."
"Questions all the time," said Mrs Harris.
"**Yak yak yak**," said Mr Harris. "I'm a busy man. I work at the Town Hall. I want to relax in the evening, not answer questions. That's *your* job."
Miss Wiss smiled. "Perhaps it's a good sign that he's interested in–"
"He's never been interested before.

telly (television): Fernseher – **yak yak yak**: bla bla bla

Tea, telly, bed. Nothing wrong with that." Mr Harris looked angry and sat closer to Miss Wiss. "I said to Mother and I'll say it to you. I **smell a rat** –" (for a horrible moment, Miss Wiss thought he had seen Herbert, who was asleep up her sleeve)– "and when Cuthbert

to smell a rat: den Braten riechen

Harris smells a rat, **heads will roll**.
Come on, Mother, **I'm off**."
Mr Harris stood up and walked to the door. He said nothing more.
Who had put a banana skin on the floor? Or was it some of Miss Wiss' magic?
"Woooaaaahhh!"
With a loud crash, Mr Harris fell on the floor.
"Oh, Cuthbert!" said Mrs Harris. "Your best suit!"
Podge's father stood up, red-faced.
"Right! That's it!" he said. "Town Hall will hear of this. Heads will roll!"

heads will roll: Köpfe werden rollen – **I'm off:** ich gehe jetzt

Mr and Mrs Harris slammed the door loudly as they left. Yes, she definitely liked children better than parents.

Miss Wiss was not often angry. But when Mr Gilbert brought a School Inspector into the classroom a few days later she was angry. The class could hear it in her voice.
"Now sit up, Class Three," she said. The School Inspector sat at a little desk at the back of the class. "Today the Inspector is with us," Miss Wiss said to the class.
The School Inspector made a sour face and wrote things on the piece of paper in front of him.
It was a quiet lesson without any magic. Hecate the Cat stayed inside Miss Wiss' bag.

Unfortunately nobody had told Herbert that the Inspector was there. Herbert wanted to **explore** the classroom.
After a few minutes of the lesson, he found a new tunnel. It was warm and dark, like a **cosy**, old-fashioned **chimney**.
Rats like chimneys. He did not know that he was **climbing** up the left leg of the School Inspector's trousers!
At first, the School Inspector **twitched**. Then he **wriggled**. Then, as Herbert **crawled** past his knee, the School Inspector jumped up.

to explore: erkunden – **cosy:** gemütlich – **chimney:** Schornstein – **to climb:** klettern – **to twitch:** zucken – **to wriggle:** sich winden – **to crawl:** krabbeln

"Oh . . . ooh . . . ," he said, hitting his leg. "What the . . . oh . . . ah . . ." He hopped around the classroom. Herbert did not like the *moving chimney* and so he crawled into the School Inspector's underpants.

"AAAARRRRRGGGGGHHHHH!" The School Inspector pulled his belt, jumped out of his trousers and ran out of the classroom.

Class Three watched the half-**naked** person sprint across the playground, out of the school gates and down the road.
Herbert was happy that the **earthquake** was over. He crawled out of the School Inspector's trousers which were lying on the classroom floor.
"Oh, Herbert," said Miss Wiss. "You've done it now."

naked: nackt – **earthquake:** Erdbeben

CHAPTER FIVE
What a Mess!

Mr Gilbert was confused. This was nothing new for Mr Gilbert. He was always confused, but this was the biggest **muddle** since he became head teacher of St Barnabas.

He had **ugly** red marks on his bald head. He could not concentrate in lessons. He had even stopped picking his nose during Assembly.

"**I'm on the horns of a dilemma**," he told Mrs Gilbert one evening. "People tell me that Miss Wiss is a disaster. Miss Gomaz and Mrs Hicks say she's a

muddle: Durcheinander – **ugly:** hässlich – **to be on the horns of a dilemma:** vor einem Dilemma stehen

troublemaker. The School Inspector says her classroom is a **health hazard**. Mr Harris says heads will roll. They all want me to send her away before the end-of-year prize-giving next week."

"**Suspend** her, Henry," said Mrs Gilbert. "What's the problem?"

"The problem is that the children of Class Three have won all the prizes this year. It's incredible. That sleepy Caroline has won the *Art Prize*, Katrina has won the '*A for Attitude' Award for Good Behaviour.* Can you believe that! Even the terrible Podge has won a certificate for his story, *The* ***Enchanted*** *Fudge Cake with a Thick Creamy Milk Chocolate Filling*. How can I say, 'Well

health hazard: Gesundheitsrisiko – **to suspend someone**: jemanden entlassen – **enchanted:** verzaubert

done Class Three and, **by the way**, I'm suspending your teacher?' "
"You must do what you think is best," said Mrs Gilbert. "But don't let others **push you around** this time."
"Of course not," said Mr Gilbert. "You know what I think about **bullying**."

"Is Mr Gilbert really going to suspend you?" asked Katrina the next day in class. "Ever since the School Inspector lost his trousers, Mr Gilbert has looked at you strangely."
"So have Miss Gomaz and Mrs Hicks," said Jack. "They look positively happy."
"My dad's smiling a lot," said Podge. "And that's never a good sign."

by the way: übrigens – **to push someone around:** jemanden herumkommandieren – **to bully:** tyrannisieren

"Don't worry about me," said Miss Wiss. "I can look after myself."

"Yeah," said Simon. "You can magic them. That would show them."

"What have I always said? No unpleasant spells," said Miss Wiss.

"Oh, Miss Wiss," said Podge. "Couldn't you just use a bit of magic – just one little spell on Mr Gilbert?"

"Maybe you could change him into a human-being," said Jack.

The children **cheered**. Miss Wiss held up her hands. Class Three were quiet.

"No," she said. "If the head teacher does not need me anymore, there's nothing I can do about it."

"Oh yes, there is," said Jack.

to cheer: anfeuern, jubeln

And that is how Class Three's great plan was created.

The prize-giving was the most important event of the year for St Barnabas. It took place on the last day before the holidays and everybody was there.
On the platform in the School Hall sat Mr Gilbert, the School Inspector, all the teachers and the Lady **Mayoress**. She was a large, impressive woman who was wearing a large, impressive hat. In the **audience** were the children and their parents.
Mr Gilbert had just finished his usual end-of-year **speech** – which was the

mayor/mayoress: Bürgermeister/Bürgermeisterin – **audience:** Publikum – **speech:** Rede

same as every other end-of-year speech for the last ten years. Even the bad jokes were not new.
"Now," he said, "I would like to ask the Lady Mayoress –" Mr Gilbert
gave a little **bow** in her direction "– to present the prizes. First, the *Art Prize* to Caroline Smith of Class Three."
There was **polite** applause as Caroline collected her prize.
"The Maths Prize goes to Jack Beddows of Class Three."
Jack collected his prize and waved to his friends from the platform.
Mr Gilbert tried not to sound shocked when he said, "The *'A for Attitude' Award for Good Behaviour* to Katrina O'Brien

bow: Verbeugung – **polite:** höflich

of Class Three." Katrina gave a little **curtsey** to the Lady Mayoress.

"And Specially Commended for his story, *The Enchanted Fudge Cake with a Thick Creamy Milk Chocolate Filling* – Peter Harris of Class Three."

Podge climbed the steps to the platform. But he did not collect his prize from the Lady Mayoress. He took the microphone from the **astonished** head teacher.

"Everyone in Class Three wants to thank Miss Wiss," he said clearly. "She's the best teacher we've ever had –"

"Give me that microphone, boy," said Mr Gilbert and **chased** Podge around the stage.

"WE HOPE SHE NEVER EVER LEAVES!" shouted Podge. "Don't we, Class Three?"

At that moment, the children of Class Three stood up and started cheering. Several of them held up banners, saying "MISS WISS IS MAGIC" and "KEEP MISS WISS".

"Stop that now, Peter," said Podge's father, as he marched towards the platform. "Just you wait till we get home."

There was a humming sound at the back of the stage where Miss Wiss was sitting quietly.

Suddenly Mr Harris **turned into** a strange pig-like animal.

"Goodness!" said Miss Gomaz. "He's a **warthog**!"

curtsey: Knicks – **astonished:** erstaunt – **to chase:** hinterherrennen, jagen – **to turn into someone or something:** sich verwandeln – **warthog:** Warzenschwein

"Surely not," said Mrs Hicks. "Warthogs don't have those funny little **tusks**. He looks more like a **wild boar** to me."
"Don't worry about that," shouted Mr Gilbert. "We have a big baaa-" In a flash, there was a sheep standing where the head teacher had been.

tusk: Stoßzahn – **wild boar:** Wildschwein

By now the school was shouting, "We want Miss Wiss! We want Miss Wiss!"
Miss Wiss stood up and Podge gave her the microphone.
"I think we should continue the prize-giving in half an hour. I'd like to see Class Three in their classroom now, please."
She walked through the audience.
Everyone was quiet.

"Phone the police, Miss Gomaz," hissed Mrs Hicks.
Miss Wiss looked over her shoulder. Suddenly Miss Gomaz and Mrs Hicks turned into two grey **geese**, making **gobbling noises**.

"That was very kind of you, Class Three," said Miss Wiss, when all the children were in the classroom. "But I'm leaving St Barnabas anyway."
There was silencc in the classroom.
"Why?" asked Katrina.
"After all that," muttered Podge.
"I go where magic is needed," said Miss Wiss. "Today you've shown that you no longer need me. You're the best class in the school."

goose/geese: Gans/Gänse – **gobbling noise:** kollerndes Geräusch

"We won't be, without you," said Caroline.

"Yes, you will," said Miss Wiss. "Wait and see."

"We'll miss you," said Jack, serious for once.

"No, you won't because . . ."

The class looked at Miss Wiss. Caroline finally stopped crying.

". . . because I'll be back," said Miss Wiss.

"When?"

"Where?"

"Next year?"

Miss Wiss held up her hands.

"I'll come back and see each one of you," she said with a smile. "When you need a bit of Miss Wiss in your life, I'll be there."

"Everyone of us?" asked Simon.

"Everyone of you," said Miss Wiss. "And I'll bring Hecate the Cat and Herbert."
Miss Wiss picked up her bag. She sat on her vacuum cleaner, like a cowboy on his horse.
"Go back to the School Hall and finish prize-giving," she said. "Everything's back to normal."

"See you soon, Class Three," she said and flew off across the playground and over the School Hall.

"Oh no," said Jack as the class walked back into the hall. "Miss Wiss has forgotten someone."
On the platform beside Mr Gilbert, the School Inspector and the Lady Mayoress, stood two grey geese.
"She'll *have* to come back now," said Katrina.
"No unpleasant spells," said Podge.
They heard a hum outside the hall.
"Gobble gobble gobble – what a mess!" said Miss Gomaz.
Jack sighed.
"I think I liked them better as geese," he said.

ALPHABETICAL WORD LIST

assembly: Schulversammlung (morgens)
armchair: Sessel
ashtray: Aschenbecher
astonished: erstaunt
audience: Publikum

barn owl: Schleiereule
bow: Verbeugung
broomstick: Besen, Besenstiel
by itself: von selbst
by the way: übrigens

caretaker: Hausmeister
china: Porzellan
chimney: Schornstein

clue: Hinweis
cosy: gemütlich
cottage: Häuschen, Hütte
crayon: Buntstift
creep: Mistkerl
curtsey: Knicks

earthquake: Erdbeben
embarrassing: peinlich
enchanted: verzaubert

football pitch: Fußballplatz
for personal greed: aus persönlicher Gier
for revenge: aus Rache

gobbling noise: kollerndes Geräusch
goose/geese: Gans/Gänse
greedy: gierig
grumpily: mürrisch

heads will roll: Köpfe werden rollen
health hazard: Gesundheitsrisiko
humming noise: leises Summen

I'm off: ich gehe jetzt

lipstick: Lippenstift

marbles: Murmeln
mayor/mayoress: Bürgermeister/
Bürgermeisterin
muddle: Durcheinander

nail varnish: Nagellack
naked: nackt
nasty: scheußlich, grässlich
nine times table: 9er-Reihe

owl: Eule

Paranormal Operatives: Fachfrauen für Übersinnliches
pellet: Kugel
pile: Haufen
polite: höflich

referee: Schiedsrichter

secret: Geheimnis
sleeve: Ärmel
speech: Rede
silly: blöd
spy: Spion
strange: seltsam

telly (television): Fernseher
thatched roof: Reetdach
to agree: zustimmen
to be on the horns of a dilemma: vor einem Dilemma stehen

to bully: tyrannisieren
to cast a spell: jemanden/etwas verzaubern
to cause trouble: Ärger machen
to chase: hinterherrennen, jagen
to cheer: anfeuern, jubeln
to climb: klettern
to complain: sich beschweren
to crawl: krabbeln
to explore: erkunden
to giggle: kichern
to groan: stöhnen
to hiss: fauchen, zischen
to mutter: murmeln
to pat: tätscheln, klopfen
to push someone around: jemanden herumkommandieren
to score (a goal): ein Tor schießen
to scratch: kratzen
to shrug: Achsel zucken

to smell a rat: den Braten riechen
to spell: buchstabieren
to stammer: stottern
to steam: dampfen
to stir: rühren
to suspend someone: jemanden entlassen
to sweep up: zusammenkehren
to tape: kleben
to turn into something or someone: sich verwandeln
to twitch: zucken
to wonder: sich fragen
to wriggle: sich winden
torch: Taschenlampe, Fackel
tusk: Stoßzahn

ugly: hässlich
unpleasant: unangenehm

vacuum cleaner: Staubsauger

warthog: Warzenschwein
waste-paper basket: Papierkorb
weird: merkwürdig
wheelbarrow: Schubkarren
whistle: Trillerpfeife
wild boar: Wildschwein
witch: Hexe

yak yak yak: bla bla bla

Terence Blacker

Miss Wiss ganz groß!

Miss-Wiss-Abenteuer 1–3

Mit Bildern von Tony Ross
Aus dem Englischen von Anu Stohner
224 Seiten (ab 6), Gulliver TB 74019

Eine Lehrerin, die hexen kann, ist erst mal unheimlich. Aber bald merken die Kinder der Sankt-Barnabas-Schule: Miss Wiss ist große Klasse! Egal, ob sie es mit eifersüchtigen Lehrerinnen, heimtückischen Katzenfängern oder Jacks rebellierendem Blinddarm zu tun hat – Miss Wiss taucht überall dort auf, wo ein kleiner Zauber vonnöten ist.

Eoin Colfer

The Legend of Spud Murphy

Illustrated by Tony Ross
Glossary included
112 Seiten (ab 10), Gulliver TB (74070)

Die ziemlich verrückte Geschichte von Spud Murphy und den Brüdern Marty und Tim – in vereinfachtem Englisch, mit Vokabeln am Ende jeder Seite.
»Extrem komisch und verrückt. Genau das Richtige, wenn du gerne Englisch sprichst und mal was Spannenderes als die Texte aus deiner ›Unit‹ lesen willst.«
Aachener Zeitung

GULLIVER www.gulliver-welten.de
Beltz & Gelberg, Postfach 10 01 54, 69441 Weinheim